GAMES + PUZZLES

DOODLING + MORE

1000 BC
500 BC
1100 BC
1400 BC
1472
1600
1800
1897
1898
1914
1926
1936
1952
1956
1959
1960
1961
1967
1970
1973
1986
1987
1991
2018

THE NIGERIAN
TIME MACHINE
ACTIVITY BOOK

MAKE WE WAKA GO!

THE PR2J3C4

ZARIA | UYO | IBADAN | ENUGU | LAGOS | ABUJA | CALABAR | BENIN | KANO | JOS | MAKURDI

THE NIGERIAN TIME MACHINE ACTIVITY BOOK

ABOUT THE 234 PROJECT

The 234 Project was founded in 2015 with the central goal to be the foremost source of information that presents a positive and factual portrait of Nigeria while also promoting the accomplishments of Nigerians around the globe.

While some of the critical narratives about Nigeria are accurate, sharing in the Nigerian experience and living her story are incomplete without also shining light on the positive and constructive attributes of our country and her citizens, attributes that truly demonstrate the greatness and brilliance of this country, often referred to as the Giant of Africa.

We are aware of the challenges facing Nigeria and the damage done to her reputation by some individuals. Notwithstanding, we are passionate and proud of the past and current achievements of Nigeria and her citizens and we are excited about what the future holds.

Akin Akinboro

Akin Akinboro
Co Founder

Mobolaji Sokunbi

Mobolaji Sokunbi
Co Founder

http://the234project.com

THE PR2J3C+

Dear Parents,

We are pleased to share this activity book that sheds light on key historical events in Nigeria with you and your child. **The Nigerian Time Machine** is the first book in the **Amazing Nigerian Explorer** series. This book includes details that we hope will inspire curiosity, inform and aid retention of your child's knowledge of one of the most diverse countries in the world.

The Nigerian Timeline will give you and your child an overview of major developments in Nigeria from the earliest mention of Nigeria in popular history to the printing of this book.

There are several activities intentionally designed to help you and your child engage, interact and connect as you discover interesting facts and information about Nigeria. (The goal of the parent-child interaction and discussion is for both parties to have fun. As you and your child read through and interact with the book, you will find opportunities for learning and fun). There are specific icons placed throughout the book to guide the learning experience. All the icons and their purposes are defined on the next page.

Finally, the book ends with a family tree that we hope will help your child connect more with his or her heritage. More copies are available for download on our website @ www.the234project.com

Be sure to also checkout our website for more information on topics covered in this book and other information on Nigeria.

This isn't just an activity book for your child

Our hope is that this activity book can also serve as a conversation piece to engage not just with your kids but also aunts, uncles, grandparents, educators, teachers, history buffs, etc. Ultimately, you don't have to be a child or a kid to appreciate and enjoy this activity book. This book is for anyone who has a desire to learn something new and would like to have fun while doing so.

Sincerely,
Akin Akinboro & Mobolaji Sokunbi

THE PR2J3C+

ABOUT THE NIGERIAN TIMELINE

Using a series of activities, your child will discover historical facts about Nigeria. The different sections in this activity book will address subjects and topics such as

- **Sports**
- **Architecture**
- **Aviation**
- **Flags**
- **Money (Currency)**
- **Family**

The answers to all the puzzles can be found in the back of this book and additional details on key facts discussed in this activity book can be found on www.the234project.com

The upper left hand corner of each page will state the type of student activity on each page. There are 11 activities in all.

MAZE RUNNER	WORD SEARCH	FIND THE DIFFERENCE
COLOR UP	CIRCLE UP	MATCH UP
DID YOU KNOW?	FILL IN THE BLANKS	CROSSWORD PUZZLE
CONNECT THE DOTS	DESIGN YOUR OWN	

 234 Facts – This icon denotes that there is currently an article on www.the234project.com that discusses this topic in depth. If you wish to learn more, we encourage you to go to www.the234project.com and search using the title in the activity book.

 Parent Connection – This icon denotes an activity we believe is best done with your child. It often requires your child to ask you a question or get your perspective on a topic.

 Timeline – This Nigerian timeline will help locate what year you're in, as it relates to the other activities.

 Meet your Tourguide – This Nigerian timeline will help locate what year you're in, as it relates to the other activities.

The Amazing Nigerian Explorer Series   **The Nigerian Time Machine**   978-0-692-98160-3

Written by: Akin Akinboro and Mobolaji Sokunbi   Illustrated by: Jasmine Sharpe   *Printed in China*

NOK
CIVILIZATION

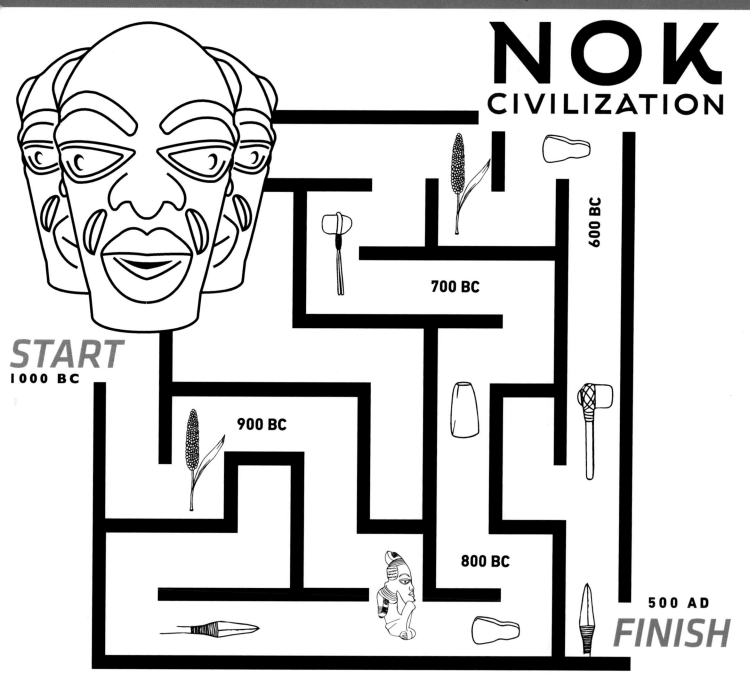

START
1000 BC

700 BC

600 BC

900 BC

800 BC

500 AD
FINISH

The terracotta sculptures that were first discovered in 1928 by Colonel Dent Young, an Englishman, near a NOK village points to the existence of an early Iron Age civilization in northern Nigeria around 1000 BC to 500 AD.

Material remains left in Northern Nigeria

 GRAINS

 TOOLS

 TERRACOTTA SCULPTURES

CERAMICS

NOK CIVILIZATION

● Jos

Taruga ●

Grains are types of grass that produce seeds that can be eaten. Wheat, Rice and Corn are the most commonly grown grains.

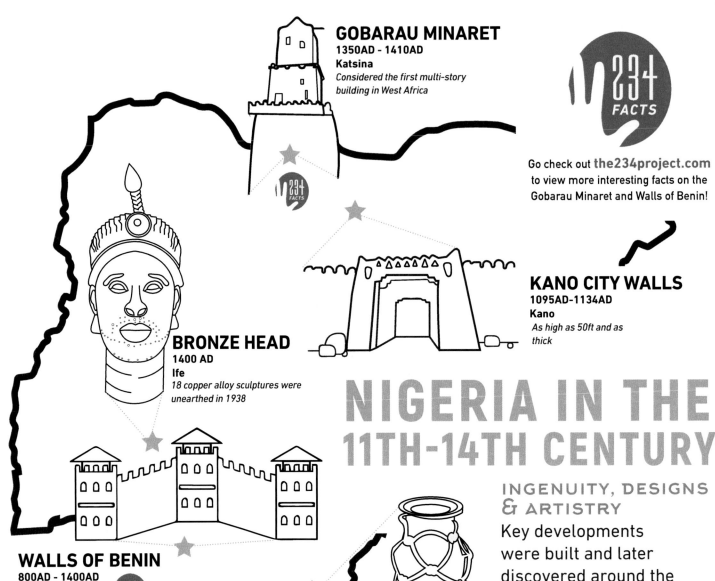

GOBARAU MINARET
1350AD - 1410AD
Katsina
Considered the first multi-story building in West Africa

234 FACTS

Go check out **the234project.com** to view more interesting facts on the Gobarau Minaret and Walls of Benin!

KANO CITY WALLS
1095AD-1134AD
Kano
As high as 50ft and as thick

BRONZE HEAD
1400 AD
Ife
18 copper alloy sculptures were unearthed in 1938

NIGERIA IN THE 11TH-14TH CENTURY

INGENUITY, DESIGNS & ARTISTRY
Key developments were built and later discovered around the country in different kingdoms

WALLS OF BENIN
800AD - 1400AD
Edo
Consumed 100x more material than the Great Pyramid of Cheops

KINGDOM OF NRI
900AD - 1900AD
Igbo-Ukwu

BRONZE IFE HEAD
The Ife Heads are believed to depict an Ooni, a powerful King of the West African kingdom of Ife (located in Osun State)

KANO CITY WALLS
Ancient Kano City Wall was a 14km (8.7miles) radius earth structure. The wall was built to protect the citizens of Kano.

BENIN WALLS
The Guinness Book of World Records (1974) describes the walls of Benin City as the **world's second largest** man-made structure after China's Great Wall

GOBARAU MINARET
The minaret was completed during the reign of the first Muslim King of Katsina, Sarkin Katsina Muhammadu Korau

KINGDOM OF NRI
Commonly viewed as one of the longest running Kingdoms in Africa. It ran from around 9th to 19th century AD. It was it it's peak during 11th to 14th Century

KEY ⭐ = LOCATION OF KINGDOMS

EUROPE

PORTUGAL

> **DID YOU KNOW:**
> There is a city
> in Portugal also
> called Lagos

AFRICA

ATLANTIC
OCEAN

Lagos

NIGERIA

Lagos

Benin
Empire ●

1472
1ST CONTACT WITH
EUROPEANS

The major trade partner for the Portuguese was
the Benin Empire (present day Edo State).

How long does it take a
ship to sail from
Lisbon, Portugal
to Lagos, Nigeria?

IN 1472	IN 2018
A) 5 days	A) 5 days
B) 7 days	B) 7 days
C) 15 days	C) 15 days
D) 20 days	D) 20 days
E) 30 days	E) 30 days

(View answer on page 31)

DID YOU KNOW?

- Lagos = Lakes in Portuguese

- The major trade partner for the Portuguese
  was the Benin Empire (Present day Edo State)

EUROPE

PORTUGAL

NIGERIA   AFRICA

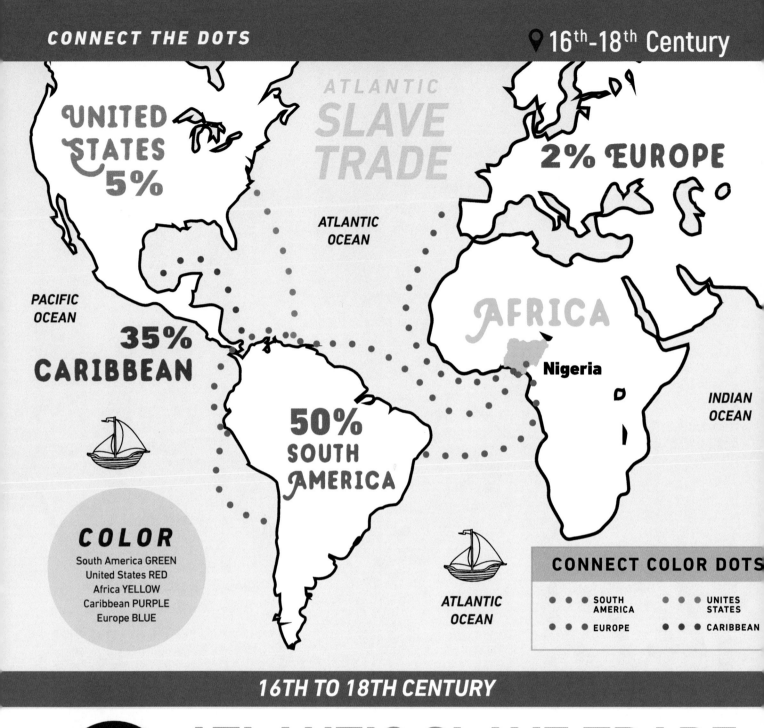

ATLANTIC SLAVE TRADE

UNITED STATES 5%

2% EUROPE

ATLANTIC OCEAN

PACIFIC OCEAN

AFRICA

Nigeria

INDIAN OCEAN

35% CARIBBEAN

50% SOUTH AMERICA

ATLANTIC OCEAN

COLOR
South America GREEN
United States RED
Africa YELLOW
Caribbean PURPLE
Europe BLUE

ATLANTIC OCEAN

CONNECT COLOR DOTS

• • • SOUTH AMERICA   • • • UNITES STATES
• • • EUROPE   • • • CARIBBEAN

16TH TO 18TH CENTURY

ATLANTIC SLAVE TRADE
OVER 12.5 MILLION SLAVES FROM AFRICA WERE
SENT TO EUROPE, CARIBBEAN, US, & SOUTH AMERICA
3.5 MILLION (30%) SLAVES WERE SENT FROM NIGERIA.

This is more than the population of present day Greece!

PARENT CONNECTION

List 3 Major non African countries where Nigerian cultures are heavily practiced

1. _____
2. _____
3. _____

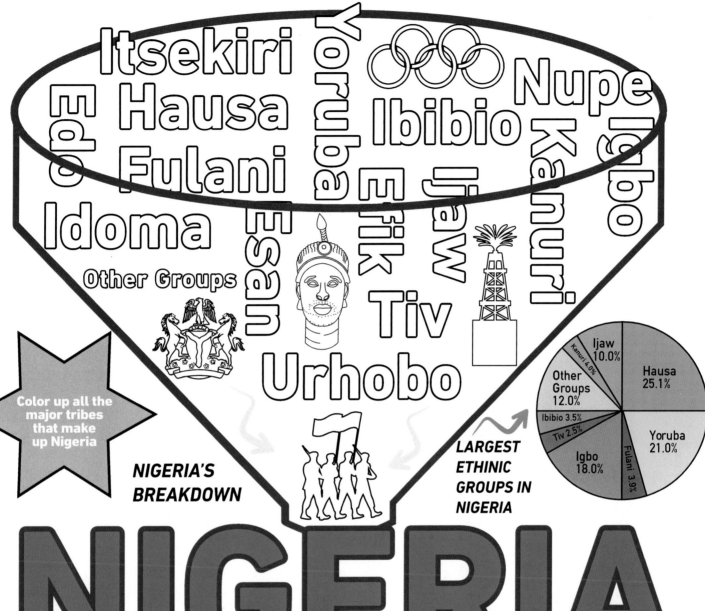

Itsekiri
Edo
Hausa
Fulani
Idoma
Other Groups
Esan
Yoruba
Ibibio
Efik
Ijaw
Tiv
Urhobo
Nupe
Kanuri
Igbo

Color up all the major tribes that make up Nigeria

NIGERIA'S BREAKDOWN

LARGEST ETHINIC GROUPS IN NIGERIA

Ijaw 10.0%
Kanuri 4.0%
Other Groups 12.0%
Ibibio 3.5%
Tiv 2.5%
Igbo 18.0%
Hausa 25.1%
Yoruba 21.0%
Fulani 3.9%

NIGERIA
1897

On January 8th, 1897 in London, Miss Shaw suggested the name "Nigeria" for the British Protectorate on the Niger River.

PARENT CONNECTION

Ask your parent their favorite thing about Nigeria!

DID YOU KNOW?

- The Niger River is the 3rd longest river in Africa(2600 miles) and it crosses 5 countries.

1898 RAILROAD IN NIGERIA

⭐ Connect the stars from 1-9 AND A-F! ⭐

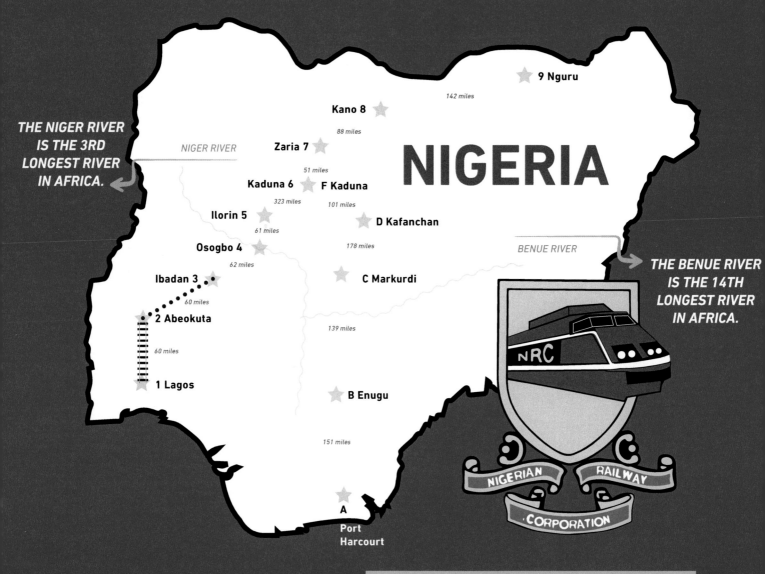

9 Nguru

142 miles

Kano 8

88 miles

Zaria 7

51 miles

THE NIGER RIVER IS THE 3RD LONGEST RIVER IN AFRICA.

NIGER RIVER

Kaduna 6   F Kaduna

323 miles   101 miles

NIGERIA

D Kafanchan

Ilorin 5

61 miles

178 miles

Osogbo 4

62 miles

BENUE RIVER

THE BENUE RIVER IS THE 14TH LONGEST RIVER IN AFRICA.

C Markurdi

Ibadan 3

60 miles

2 Abeokuta

139 miles

60 miles

1 Lagos

B Enugu

151 miles

A

Port Harcourt

The Nigerian Railway Corporation traces its history to the year 1898, when the first railroad in Nigeria was constructed by the British colonial government.

DID YOU KNOW?

- The bridge over the Benue River was first opened in 1932.
- The bridge over the Niger River was first opened after 1916.

Have you ever been on a train? Trains are super cool!

1914 AMALGAMATION OF NIGERIA

On the 1st of January 1914, Nigeria became a single country. The Northern and Southern Protectorates were joined together.

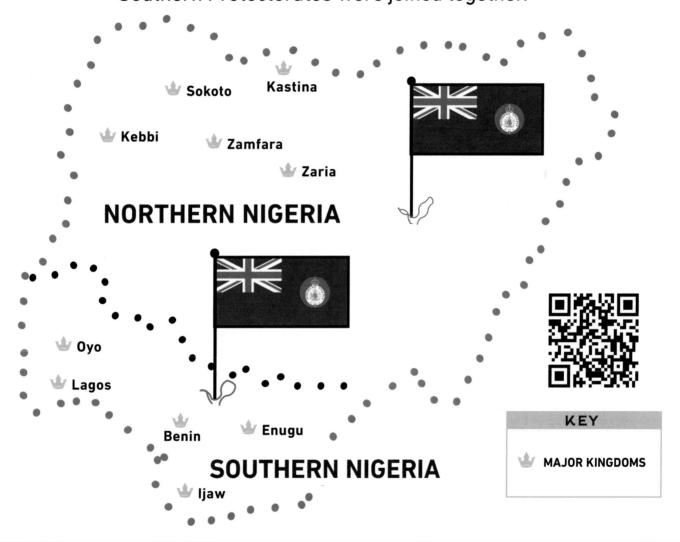

NORTHERN NIGERIA

👑 Sokoto   👑 Kastina
👑 Kebbi   👑 Zamfara
👑 Zaria

SOUTHERN NIGERIA

👑 Oyo
👑 Lagos
👑 Benin   👑 Enugu
👑 Ijaw

KEY
👑 MAJOR KINGDOMS

FOLLOW DIRECTIONS:

1. Connect black dots representing the separation of Southern and Northern Nigeria
2. Connect red dots representing Southern Nigeria
3. Connect green dots representing Northern Nigeria
4. Color in the whole shape with your favorite color representing Nigeria coming together

NLLYWOOD

Nigeria's Movie Industry

Orlando Martins

Pioneering Nigerian film and stage actor

234 FACTS

Nollywood employs over

1 million people

Nollywood makes more than HOLLYWOOD in Los Angeles, California.

40 movies per week

1926

In 1926, the 1st movie featured a Nigerian in a lead speaking role

Go check out **the234project.com** to view more interesting facts on Nigeria's Movie Industry!

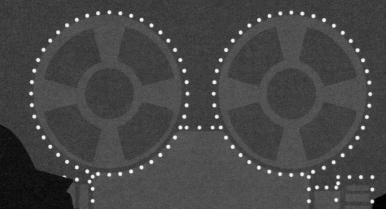

PARENT CONNECTION

Ask your parent What was your favorite TV show growing up?

Connect The Dots!

What is your favorite Nollywood movie? Who is your favorite Actor or Actress?

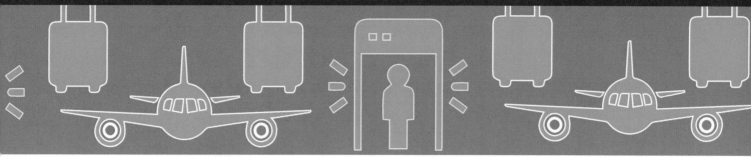

THE 1ST AIRPORT
IN NIGERIA

Mallam Aminu Kano International Airport in Kano, 1936

The first airport is named after Aminu **Kano**. He was a politician from the northern part of the country. In the 1940s, he led a socialist movement in opposition to British rule

C P U B L K Y V B X W Y K U R U N B R U

W U Y Z M H S R B B M K D A S A B A A S

Q E O M E N U G U C A R A B A L A C B O

S J R W P S L A G O S E L N V N B Z U K

W H I L Q E Q D W I O B B O O B C N J O

L C Y X I M P O R T H A R C O U R T A T

U Y G J H H I O O A X C L Y K D P H Z O

D T L E S T U D E L J S I V X N P A L K

Find the cities with International Airports in Nigeria

Abuja   Calabar
Kano   Port Harcourt
Lagos   Enugu

°Kano

°Abuja

°Enugu

Lagos
°
Port Harcourt° °Calabar *(As of 2018)*

NIGERIA
1ST PARTICIPATED IN HELSINKI OLYMPIC
GAMES

1952

Nigerian athletes have appeared in every edition of the Summer Olympic Games, with the exception of the 1976 Summer Olympics in Montreal due to the withdrawal of at least 20 African Countries including Nigeria.

1ST MEDALIST WAS NOJIM MAIYEGUM

CHIOMA AJUNWA: 1ST TO WIN GOLD IN 1996

Atlanta 1996
3588

23 TOTAL MEDALS WON

1ST GOLD WON 1992

1ST MEDAL WON 1964

CIRCLE THE SPORTS YOU LIKE TO PLAY!

Most Nigerians love soccer. What is your favorite sport?

1952

90%

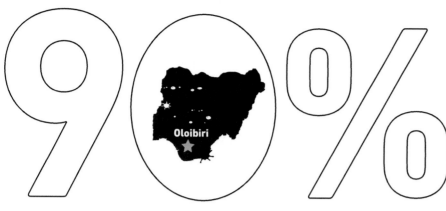

Oloibiri

OF NIGERIA'S EXPORT IS OIL

DID YOU KNOW?

Shell started business in Nigeria in 1930's as Shell D'Arcy.

In 1956, Shell discovered the first commercial oil field in the country.

Oloibiri Field is an oil field in Nigeria. This field is about 13.75 sq kilometers (5.31 sq mi) and lies in a swamp.

1 mile= 1.60934 kilomers

This is about the size of 1,500 soccer fields!

OIL MAKES LIFE A LITTLE EASIER!

FILL IN THE BLANKS WITH THE NAME OF EACH ITEM THAT WORKS WITH OIL.

1956 QUEEN ELIZABETH VISITS NIGERIA

The Queen spent 3 weeks in Nigeria.

January 28th - February 16th
This trip included trips to
Lagos, Kaduna, Enugu,
Port-Harcourt Jos.

Major Royal figures In Nigeria

1. ALAKE OF EGBA
2. OBA OF BENIN
3. ALAFIN OF OYO
4. SULTAN OF SOKOTO
5. EMIR OF KANO
6. OBA OF IFE

Create your own postcard showing
your visit to Nigeria!

Queen Elizabeth II has ruled longer
than any other King or Queen in
British history. She became Queen on
February 6th, 1952.

FLAGS OF NIGERIA

Flag of the Royal Niger Company
(1888-1899)

Flag of the Northern Nigeria
Protectorate *(1900-1914)*

Flag of the Southern Nigeria
Protectorate *(1900-1914)*

Flag of the Colony and Protectorate
of Nigeria *(1914-1960)*

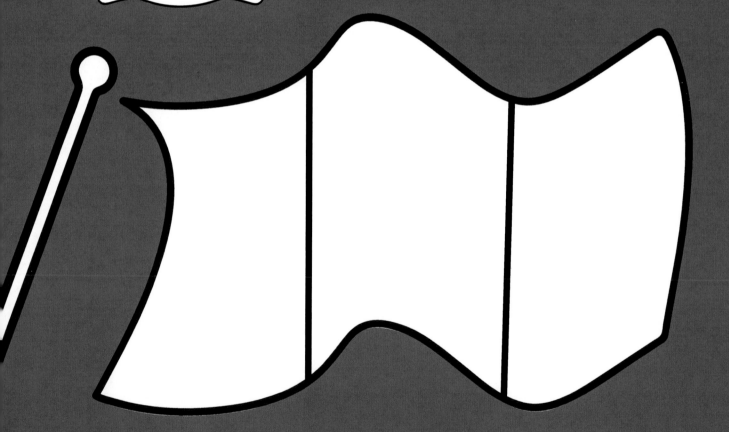

Do you know the colors of Nigeria's flag?

1959

The flag design was made in 1959, but was first officially used on the 1st of October in 1960, Nigeria's Independence Day.

1959 AIRED
FIRST TELEVISION STATION

Television (TV) began broadcasting on October 31st, 1959 under the name Western Nigerian Government Broadcasting Corporation (WNTV).

List your favorite tv shows here:

_____

1. _____

2. _____

3. _____

4. _____

5. _____

SPOT THE DIFFERENCE BETWEEN THE 2 PICTURES

PARENT CONNECTION

Ask your parent:
What was the first TV SHOW your parent watched when they were younger?

Nigeria
INDEPENDENCE

ST PRESIDENT
DR. NNAMDI
AZIKIWE

INDEPENDENT
NATION

OCTOBER 1,1960

Nigeria gained independence from the United Kingdom. Nigeria gained independence from the United Kingdom on the 1st of October in 1960. An Executive Council, made up entirely of Nigerians, was led by Prime Minister, Alhaji Sir Abubakar Tafawa Balewa.

1961 TAFAWA BALEWA VISITS U.S

Tafawa Balewa was the 1st Prime Minister of Nigeria and he had an official state visit to the United States in 1961.

Tafawa Balewa served from 1957 to 1966.
He worked well with leaders of other countries.
He is the face of the 5 Naira currency note.
Tafawa Balewa had a teaching certificate.

1960

Tafawa Balewa Time Magazine cover launched on December 5th, 1960.

PARENT CONNECTION

Ask your parent:
Which teacher had the most impact in their life? How?

1967 1970 BIAFRAN CIVIL WAR

Biafran War was a war fought between the government of Nigeria and the secessionist state of Biafra. Biafra represented nationalist aspirations of the **Igbo people.**

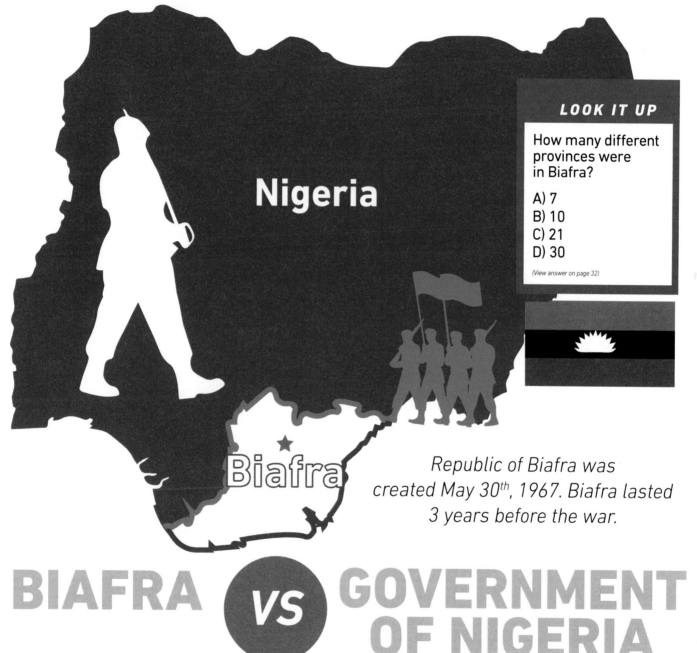

Nigeria

Biafra

LOOK IT UP

How many different provinces were in Biafra?

A) 7
B) 10
C) 21
D) 30

(View answer on page 32)

Republic of Biafra was created May 30th, 1967. Biafra lasted 3 years before the war.

BIAFRA **VS** GOVERNMENT OF NIGERIA

PARENT CONNECTION

Ask your parent:
Do you know anyone from the Biafra provinces below? Highlight each one.

Aba Owerri Umuahia Orlu Ikot-Ekpene Uyo Eket

Ogoja Calabar Enugu Oji-river Awka Onitsha Nnewi Okigwe

Annang Abakiliki Yenegoa Ahoada Degema Port-Harcourt

1973

CENTRAL BANK OF NIGERIA
INTRODUCES
NEW MONEY

On the January 1st, 1973, the Central Bank of Nigeria introduced the 50 kobo and the 1, 5, 10 and 20 naira.

MATCH MONEY TO CORRECT COUNT

50 KOBO
Issued in 1989

₦500 NAIRA
Issued in 2001

₦1000 NAIRA
Issued in 2005

₦100 NAIRA
Issued in 1999

₦200 NAIRA
Issued in 2000

₦50 NAIRA
Issued in 1991

₦20 NAIRA
Issued in 1973

FOOTBALL (SOCCER), THE NATION'S HEART BEAT.

CONTINENTAL CHAMPIONSHIPS

SUPER EAGLES
AFRICAN CUP OF NATIONS

Won 3 Championships!
(1980, 1994, 2013)

Won the most championships of any African country!

SUPER FALCONS CAF
WOMEN'S CHAMPIONSHIPS

Won 9 Championships!
(1995, 1998, 2000, 2002, 2004, 2006, 2010, 2014, 2016)

WORLD CHAMPIONSHIPS

Won more than any country in the world!

11

U17 SOCCER TEAM
(GOLDEN EAGLETS)

Won 5 Championships!
(1985, 1993, 2007, 2013, 2015)

GOLD IN THE
1996 OLYMPICS

START ▶

Can you beat our time of 2 minutes to get to the soccer ball?

IN 1986 WOLE SOYINKA WAS THE 1ST AFRICAN TO WIN THE NOBEL PRIZE IN LITERATURE

Wole Soyinka is a Nigerian playwright and poet. Soyinka was born into a Yoruba family in Abeokuta. After studying in Nigeria and the UK, he worked with the Royal Court Theatre in London. He went on to write plays that were produced in both countries, in theaters and on radio.

WRITE YOUR OWN POEM

My hair is .... *like* ....

My face is .... *as* ....

My nose is .... *like* ....

My body is .... *like* ....

DUFUNA CANOE FOUND

Dufuna Canoe is a canoe discovered in 1987 by a Fulani cattle **herdsman** a few kilometers from the village of Dufuna, not far from the Komadugu Gana River, in Yobe State, Nigeria.

It is the **oldest** boat to be discovered in **Africa**.

Radiocarbon dating of a sample of charcoal found near the site dates the canoe at 8500 to 8000 years old, linking the site to Lake **Mega Chad**.

Across

3 Canoe Name

5 What lake can you link the canoe to?

Down

1 What country was the canoe found in?

2 _____ found the canoe

4 This canoe is the _____

HINT
Look for clues in the paragraphs above.

1990 3RD MAINLAND BRIDGE WAS BUILT

The Third Mainland Bridge is the longest of three bridges connecting Lagos Island to the mainland, the other two being the Eko and Carter Bridges.

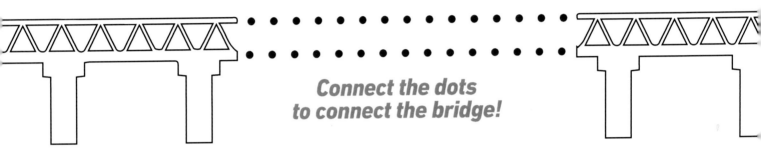

Connect the dots to connect the bridge!

This bridge is 11.8km = 7.33miles!

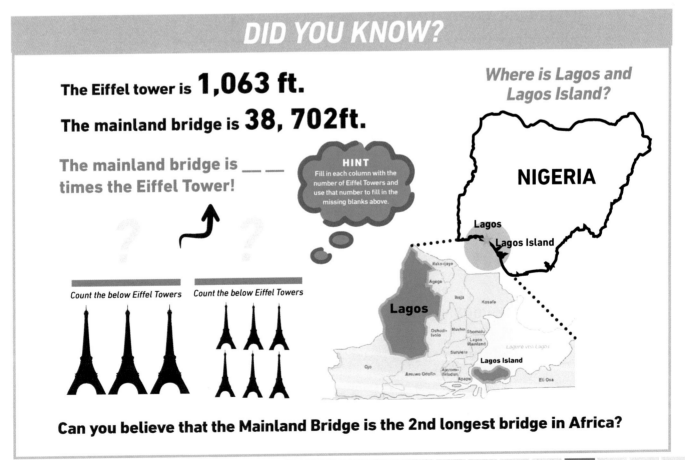

DID YOU KNOW?

The Eiffel tower is **1,063 ft.**

The mainland bridge is **38, 702ft.**

The mainland bridge is __ __ times the Eiffel Tower!

HINT
Fill in each column with the number of Eiffel Towers and use that number to fill in the missing blanks above.

Where is Lagos and Lagos Island?

NIGERIA

Lagos

Lagos Island

Lagos

Lagos Island

Count the below Eiffel Towers

Count the below Eiffel Towers

Can you believe that the Mainland Bridge is the 2nd longest bridge in Africa?

1991

NIGERIA'S CAPITAL MOVES TO ABUJA

After 77 years of Lagos serving as the seat of government, the central government moved to Abuja.

ABUJA

PARENT CONNECTION

List the names of the cities in Nigeria that your parents have been to.

_____

_____

_____

_____

_____

NIGERIA

★ **Abuja**
Founded in 1975
Population of 2 million
Location of Aso Rock

Lagos

• Founded in 15th Century
• Population of 25 million
• Primary Sea Port for Nigeria

ASK YOURSELF

If you could live anywhere where would it be?

★ 1991

Miss World Agbani Darego

Agbani Darego, is a Nigerian model and beauty queen, best known as the first native African to win Miss World in 2001.

NIGERIA

Port Harcourt

234 FACTS

Go check out **the234project.com** to view more interesting facts on Agbani Darego!

DID YOU KNOW?

Grace Atinuke is known to be the first Miss Nigeria. She was crowned in 1957.

Miss World

NIGERIA, WHERE WE ARE TODAY

POPULATION
185 MILLION, 7th in the world

LANGUAGES
#!& 517 LANGUAGES, 3rd most in the world

Top 20 Countries: HIGHEST PERCENTAGE OF POPULATION Under 18 Years Old

```
R A K A O M I Y O B E M J I G A W A K A
I E R A N N K N U S O O Q A D A M A W A
V B V A D A D E L T A B U Y R M T A E O
E A A I F U M O B W N I G E R S R D N Y
R Y I J R M N B F B I A Q S I A O R O O
S E H E U S A A R Y I W O N S G O M B E
O L C U G B S Z N A G K A A A B A R A T
G S U N U C A O B J O A N U A E T A L P
A A A E N A B I R T K I T I K E O N A K
L D B B E E A G O C A R A W K O G U N J
```

Find the states within Nigeria

ABIA	BAUCHI	DELTA	GOMBE	KATSINA	NASARAWA	OYO	YOBE
ABUJA	BAYELSA	EBONYI	IMO	KEBBI	NIGER	PLATEAU	TARABA
ADAMAWA	BENUE	EDO	JIGAWA	KOGI	OGUN	RIVERS	ZAMFARA
AKWA-IBOM	BORNO	EKITI	KADUNA	KWARA	ONDO	SOKOTO	
ANAMBRA	CROSS-RIVER	ENUGU	KANO	LAGOS	OSUN		

Nigeria has the largest number of internet users in Africa **OVER 90 MILLION**

Nigeria has 1 of the *HIGHEST TWIN BIRTH RATES* in the world

Forbes
RICHEST BLACK MAN
Industrialist
Aliko Dangote is worth an estimated **$12 Billion**

RICHEST BLACK WOMAN
Business
Mogul Folorunsho Alakija is worth an estimated **$1.6 Billion**

DESIGN YOUR OWN

GREAT GRANDMA NAME

GREAT GRANDPA NAME

GREAT GRANDMA NAME

GREAT GRANDPA NAME

GREAT GRANDMA NAME

GREAT GRANDPA NAME

GREAT GRANDMA NAME

GREAT GRANDPA NAME

GRANDMA NAME

GRANDPA NAME

GRANDMA NAME

GRANDPA NAME

FATHER NAME

MOTHER NAME

Place a photograph
or draw a pic
of your family member in
each bubble!

Family
Tree

YOUR NAME

Page 7

How long does it take to sail from Lisbon, Portugal to Lagos, Nigeria?

Distance is about 3512nm (Nautical Miles)

Most ships in 1472 traveled around 5knots, it will take=

30 days

Most ships in 2017 travel around 21knots, it will take=

7 days

Page 8

List 3 major Non African countries where Nigerian cultures are heavily practiced?

Brazil

Jamaica

Caribbean Islands

Page 10

Route to connect the dots

Page 11

Route to connect the dots

Page 12

Route to connect the dot

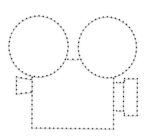

Page 13

```
C P U B L K Y V B X W Y K U R U N B R U
W U Y Z M H S R B B M K D A S A B A A S
Q E O M E N U G U C A R A B A L A C B O
S J R W P S L A G O S E L N V N B Z U K
W H I L Q E Q D W I O B B O O B C N J O
L C Y X I M P O R T H A R C O U R T A T
U Y G J H H I O O A X C L Y K D P H Z O
D T L E S T U D E L J S I V X N P A L K
```

Page 15

List items that are associated with oil

Gas cooker
Generator
Truck/Trailer/Lorry

Car
Petroleum Jelly
Airplane

Page 18

Page 21

How many different provinces were there in Biafra?

21 Provinces

Page 22

Match up

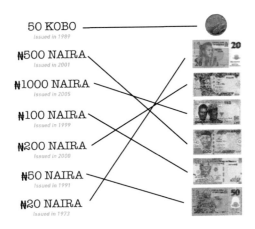

Crossword:

1. africa
2. herdsman
3. dufuna
4. oldest
5. megachad

Page 23

START ▶

Page 26

The mainland bridge is __ __ times the Eiffel Tower.

3rd Mainland Bridge is 36

Page 29

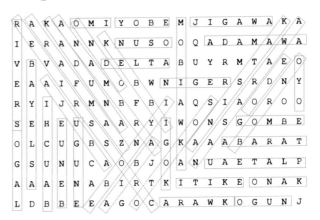

MADE IN CHINA

THE AMAZING NIGERIAN EXPLORER SERIES

THE NIGERIAN TIME MACHINE ACTIVITY BOOK

GAMES • PUZZLES  DOODLING + MORE

This fun educational book is packed full of imaginative and exciting activities that will help kids learn and discover unique historical events and key major developments about Nigeria.

In this book, Parents and Kids will embark on an entertaining journey across The Nigerian Timeline and discover amazing details about the country referred to as the "Giant of Africa".

Akin Akinboro and Mobolaji Sokunbi (left to right) are the Co-Founders of The 234 Project. They first met nearly 20 years ago at a time when each person was much involved in the African Students Association (ASA) at their respective universities. In 2015, they got together and launched The 234 Project with the goal to be the foremost source of information that presents a positive and factual portrait of Nigeria while also promoting the accomplishments of Nigerians around the globe.

$19.99
ISBN 978-0-692-98160-3

9 780692 981603
51999>

Made in the USA
Coppell, TX
18 April 2022